I Can't
FAIR ISLE
KNITTING

Follow Sheila G. Joynes's thorough instructions for Fair Isle knitting, and soon you'll finish a beautiful Garden Cowl. After that, five colorful Fair Isle hats for the family await your discovery! As a special feature, you can personlize the color keys, making it easy to use the yarn colors of your choice. To inspire you, we've shown two color versions for most of these fun projects. Everything you need to know about Fair Isle knitting is here. Just think how thrilling it will be to say, "I can't believe I'm Fair Isle Knitting!"

LEISURE ARTS, INC.
Little Rock, Arkansas

MEET THE DESIGNER

Sheila G. Joynes says, "Friends and family describe my relationship to Fair Isle knitting as 'She paints with yarn.'"

Sheila's knitting journey began when she was a teenager, but she was fascinated by color long before then. She says, "As a small child, I would spend hours studying a book of my grandmother's called World Famous Paintings. Years later, I graduated from the University of Washington with an Art Education degree. It provided me with an opportunity to focus on my love of color and fiber. Watercolor, fiber art, and photography were my favorite classes. I incorporated art in most of my lesson plans as a teacher and a volunteer."

Sheila's family has played an important part in her design career. "Throughout my adventures with fiber arts," she says, "my primary focus has been on knitting. I began the designing leg of this journey when my son became a teenager and wanted his sweaters to be custom-designed and not recreated from a pattern as it was originally published.

"I've taught at local yarn shops over the years. Currently, I am fortunate enough to teach at Debbie Macomber's A Good Yarn Shop in Port Orchard, WA. I now lead knitting classes and specialize in two-handed Fair Isle Technique. The classes in Fair Isle are very popular and fill up quickly. I love creating color designs and I enjoy spreading my love for Fair Isle color.

"I look for my color motivation in nature and enjoy taking nature and gardening photographs. I tell my students if you pick colors from nature you can't go wrong. The two things that go with me everywhere are my knitting and my camera."

THANK YOU

I want to say a special thank you to my wonderful husband Harry for his love, patience and support. I would also like to thank Debbie Macomber, Sandy Payne, Cindy Novita-Mason, and my lovely children Tamiko and Todd. Many friends and family members have encouraged me along this knitting journey and I wish I had room to mention their names. I love and thank them all.

I would also like to thank test knitters Elizabeth Bartlett, Betty Jesch, and Audrey Roos, as well as Conny Johannesson, our contributing photographer for technique.

Sheila G. Joynes

—Sheila G. Joynes

HISTORY

Traditional Fair Isle is a knitting technique used to create patterns with multiple colors. The name originated from a tiny island called Fair Isle from an area of the Shetland Islands in the furthermost part of Scotland. Fair Isle gained in popularity when the Prince of Wales wore a Fair Isle sweater to a public event in 1921.

Traditional Fair Isle patterns use only two colors per row in which the yarns are stranded across the back of the work. The islanders found using more than two colors per row produced a bulky and unsightly fabric. Fair Isle patterns are mainly worked in the round with the knit stitch.

GETTING STARTED

The best way to learn the technique is to start with a simple project. The projects are arranged by level of Fair Isle difficulty, so our first project is the Garden Cowl (see Fair Isle skill level chart below and project skill level chart, page 34). It has a limited number of color changes and gives you an opportunity to practice your technique, beginning with the ribbing. If you want to start with a hat instead of the Cowl, please review the instructions for Working With Multiple Colors, page 6, before you begin. We included step-by-step instructions with photos to help you learn how to Fair Isle knit with ease. Soon you will be saying, "I Can't Believe I'm Fair Isle Knitting!"

FAIR ISLE SKILL LEVEL

●○○○ **BEGINNER**	Projects that have a limited number of color changes and simple color patterns.
●●○○ **EASY**	Projects that have a limited number of color changes and simple as well as slightly larger color patterns.
●●●○ **INTERMEDIATE**	Projects that have many color changes with simple to slightly more complex color patterns.
●●●● **EXPERIENCED**	Projects that have many color changes with complex color patterns that can include decreases.

TOOLS

You will need a circular knitting needle, double pointed knitting needles for the hats in the same size as the circular needle, stitch marker(s), tapestry or yarn needle, ruler or knitting needle gauge tool, small plastic bags, and a chart holder with a magnet *(Photo 1)*. A page protector can also be used for the chart.

Photo 1

PREPARATION

Preparation is very important for your Fair Isle project. Make a color copy of the chart page. After deciding on your colors, write the color of the yarn for each color listed under the key. Cut a sample of yarn and tape it under the color. Put the page on a chart holder and lay a magnet on it to keep your place *(Photo 2)*. The chart holder can be inserted in a page protector with the magnet on the outside, if desired.

Photo 2

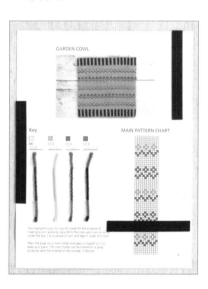

If your yarn comes in a hank, roll it into a pull skein. On the back of each yarn label, write the name of the color, such as MC for Main Color. Tape a small snip of yarn on the back of the label. Make a small diagonal cut across one of the bottom corners of a small plastic bag for your yarn to feed through. Place each skein and the label in the bag and pull the strand through the hole; seal the bag *(Photo 3)*.

Photo 3

Garden Cowl

Refer to Preparation, page 3, before you begin.

Project: ◼◼◻◻ **EASY**
Fair Isle pattern: ●○○○ **BEGINNER**

Finished Size: 22" (56 cm) around and
11" (28 cm) high

version 2

MATERIALS
Medium Weight Yarn
Version 1
[1.75 ounces, 110 yards
(50 grams, 101 meters) per skein]:
   Two skeins of MC (Grey)
   One skein **each** of the following colors:
   CC1 (Pink), CC2 (Green), CC3 (Purple)
Version 2
[3.5 ounces, 223 yards
(100 grams, 204 meters) per skein]:
   One skein **each** of the following colors:
   MC (Burgundy), CC1 (Pink), CC2 (Jade),
   CC3 (Aqua)
16" (40.5 cm) length circular knitting needle,
   size 6 (4 mm) **or** size needed for gauge
Marker
Yarn needle

GAUGE: In Stockinette Stitch,
      24 sts and 28 rows = 4" (10 cm)

WORKING WITH MULTIPLE COLORS

The Fair Isle pattern in all of the projects is worked in the round with the **right** side facing, knitting every stitch. Since the right side is always facing, it's easy to see your pattern develop.

There are several knitting methods of holding your yarn for Fair Isle stranding, but we will concentrate on the **two-hand stranded technique** for a couple of reasons. This method will prevent the two yarns you are using from tangling and twisting. It is a faster technique, because you don't have to stop and untangle your yarns. It's great for carrying your yarn across the back without much effort and you may find it very rhythmic.

When working a Fair Isle pattern, you'll need to determine which yarn is the dominant pattern color and which color is the background color *(Photo 4)*.

Photo 4

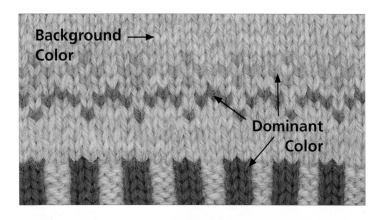

You will be using both hands to work across each color pattern round. Always place the dominant pattern color strand in your left hand (picking, or Continental style) and background color strand in your right hand (throwing, or English style) *(Photo 5)*. In this project, the contrasting color is always the dominant pattern color and the main color is always the background color.

Photo 5

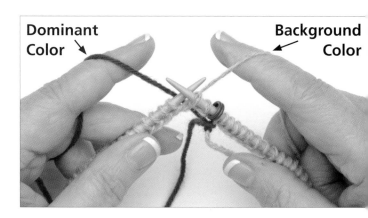

Now you're ready to begin your project!

BOTTOM RIBBING

Cast on 132 sts with MC using your circular needle.

Join CC3 to the tail of MC with a temporary knot near the needle to anchor the yarn *(see example in Photo 5)*.

Place a marker before the first stitch to mark the beginning of the round *(see Markers, page 35)*, and make sure that the cast on stitches are not twisted *(see Circular Needles, page 36)*.

Now it's time to begin knitting with both hands.

Rnd 1: P2, K2 with CC3, P2 with MC.

Notice that the left hand strand comes from underneath the right hand strand *(Photo 6)*. This will make your pattern color show up more and become prominent in the design.

Photo 6

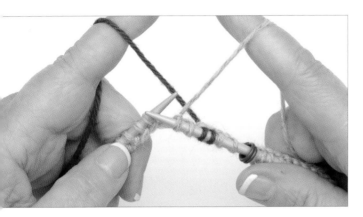

The yarn colors carried across the wrong side of your piece are called *floats*. It is important to keep an **even tension** when maintaining your floats. With a couple of the following tricks, you shouldn't have any problems. You will want to keep the stitches on your right needle spread out as much as the approximate gauge *(Photo 7)* and make sure your float yarn is carried flat against the back of your work. Make sure the floats aren't so loose that the stitches at the end of the color sections are enlarged or pulled too tight, causing your work to pucker.

Photo 7

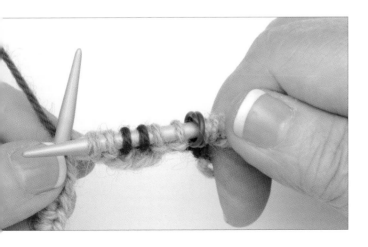

Continue to work in ribbing on Rnd 1 as follows: K2 with CC3, ★ P2 with MC, K2 with CC3; repeat from ★ to end of rnd.

Rnd 2: ★ P2 with MC, K2 with CC3; repeat from ★ to end of rnd.

Rnds 3-5: Repeat Rnd 2, 3 times.

The stitches on the right side should look smooth and even *(Photo 8)* and each float should be carried flat across the wrong side **without** crossing one another *(Photo 9)*.

Photo 8

Photo 9

Rnds 6-10: Repeat Rnd 2, 5 times.

Cut CC3 at the end of Rnd 10, leaving approximately a 6" (15 cm) length to weave in later.

BODY

Written instructions, as well as a chart on page 9, are provided for the main color pattern *(see Following A Chart, page 35)*. You can refer back and forth from the instructions to the chart until you feel comfortable following a chart.

In order to condense the instructions in an easy-to-read form, the number of stitches to knit is followed by the color to use, and they are separated by a slash. For example, K2/MC means you are to knit 2 stitches with MC.

Add colors as needed, and cut yarn after all of the rounds in that color section have been worked, leaving a long enough end to weave in later.

Rnds 1-4: Knit with MC to end of rnd.

Rnd 5: K2/MC, K1/CC2, ★ K3/MC, K1/CC2; repeat from ★ to last st, K1/MC.

Rnd 6: ★ K1/MC, K1/CC2; repeat from ★ to end of rnd.

Rnd 7: ★ K1/CC2, K3/MC; repeat from ★ to end of rnd; cut CC2.

Rnd 8: K2/MC, K1/CC1, ★ K3/MC, K1/CC1; repeat from ★ to last st, K1/MC.

Rnd 9: ★ K1/MC, K1/CC1; repeat from ★ to end of rnd.

Rnd 10: K2/MC, K1/CC1, ★ K3/MC, K1/CC1; repeat from ★ to last st, K1/MC; cut CC1.

Rnds 11-15: Knit with MC to end of rnd.

Rnd 16: K2/MC, K1/CC2, ★ K3/MC, K1/CC2; repeat from ★ to last st, K1/MC.

Rnd 17: ★ K1/MC, K1/CC2; repeat from ★ to end of rnd.

Rnd 18: ★ K1/CC2, K3/MC; repeat from ★ to end of rnd; cut CC2.

Rnd 19: K2/MC, K1/CC3, ★ K3/MC, K1/CC3; repeat from ★ to last st, K1/MC.

Rnd 20: ★ K1/MC, K1/CC3; repeat from ★ to end of rnd.

Rnd 21: K2/MC, K1/CC3, ★ K3/MC, K1/CC3; repeat from ★ to last st, K1/MC; cut CC3.

Rnds 22-26: Knit with MC to end of rnd.

Rnds 27-54: Repeat Rnds 5-26 once, then repeat Rnds 5-10 once **more**.

Rnds 55-58: Knit with MC to end of rnd.

TOP RIBBING

Rnds 1-10: ★ P2/MC, K2/CC3; repeat from ★ to end of rnd.

Bind off in Ribbing with MC.

Weave in all loose yarn ends.

Block Cowl *(see Blocking, page 39)*.

CONGRATULATIONS!

Now you are ready to continue on your Fair Isle journey. Have fun knitting and enjoying the wonderful color combinations you can use in Fair Isle. My hope is you will grow to love Fair Isle knitting as much as I do.

GARDEN COWL

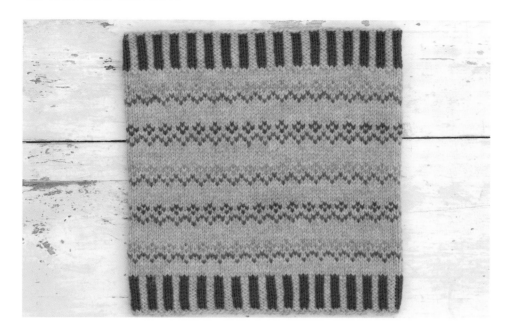

Key

 MC

 CC1

 CC2

CC3

MAIN PATTERN CHART

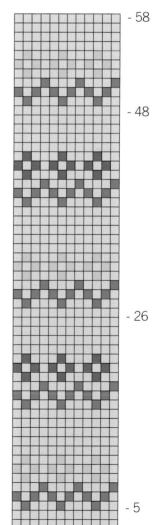

- 58

- 48

- 26

- 5

- 1

Columbia River Ear Flap Hat

Project: ◨◧◻◻ **EASY**
Fair Isle pattern: ●●○○ **EASY**

This is a great project for wearing on winter slopes or to give to a teenager who likes skateboarding. After the Ear Flaps are made, the Hat is knit in the round on a circular needle in a small 2-color Fair Isle pattern. The crown shaping is worked in the main color, changing to double points as needed.

Size: Fits head circumference of 18{20, 22}"/
45.5{51, 56} cm

Size Note: Instructions are given for the smallest size with the medium and large sizes in braces { }. When only one number is given, it applies to all sizes.

version 2

MATERIALS
Medium Weight Yarn
Version 1
[3.5 ounces, 223 yards
(100 grams, 204 meters) per skein]:
   One skein **each** of the following colors:
   MC (Grey), CC (Blue)
Version 2
[3 ounces, 158 yards
(85 grams, 144 meters) per skein]:
   One skein **each** of the following colors:
   MC (Sage), CC (Rose)
16" (40.5 cm) length circular knitting needle,
   size 6 (4 mm) **or** size needed for gauge
Set of 4 double pointed knitting needles in
   6" (15 cm) length, size 6 (4 mm) **or** size needed
   for gauge
Marker
Yarn needle
Optional: stitch holder

GAUGE: In Stockinette Stitch,
         21 sts = 4" (10 cm)
         in color pattern,
         24 sts and 28 rnds = 4" (10 cm)

Gauge Swatch:
Cast on 34 sts with MC using a double pointed needle.
Work all right side rows for 28 rows *(see Fair Isle Gauge Swatch, page 35)*.
Bind off all sts.

Techniques used:
- M1P *(Figs. 8a & b, page 38)*
- K2 tog *(Fig. 9, page 38)*

EAR FLAP

Cast on 6 sts with MC using your double pointed needle.

Row 1 AND ALL RIGHT SIDE ROWS: Knit to end of row.

Row 2: K2, M1P, P2, M1P, K2: 8 sts total.

Row 4: K2, M1P, P4, M1P, K2: 10 sts total.

Row 6: K2, M1P, P6, M1P, K2: 12 sts total.

Row 8: K2, M1P, P8, M1P, K2: 14 sts total.

Row 10: K2, M1P, P 10, M1P, K2: 16 sts total.

Row 12: K2, M1P, P 12, M1P, K2: 18 sts total.

Row 14: K2, M1P, P 14, M1P, K2: 20 sts total.

Row 16: K2, M1P, P 16, M1P, K2: 22 sts total.

Row 18: K2, P 18, K2.

Repeat Rows 17 and 18 until Ear Flap measures 2½{2¾, 3}"/6.5{7, 7.5} cm from the beginning, ending by working a **wrong** side row.

Cut yarn. You can leave the stitches on the double pointed needle or slip them onto a stitch holder.

Make a second Ear Flap, but do **not** cut yarn.

BAND

Use the Backward Loop Cast On method to connect the Ear Flaps, by making a loop and placing it on the needle *(Fig. 1)*.

Fig. 1

Foundation Rnd: Using your circular needle and continuing with MC, knit across the second Ear Flap, cast on 36{44, 50} sts for the front, knit across first Ear Flap, cast on 20{22, 26} sts for the back: 100{110, 120} sts total.

You will join and begin working in the round. Place a marker before the first stitch to mark the beginning of the round *(see Markers, page 35)*, and make sure that the cast on stitches are not twisted *(see Circular Needles, page 36)*.

Rnds 1-3: Purl to end of rnd.

BODY

Knit 9{11,15} rnds.

Knit 21 rnds following Chart Rows 1-21, page 15, adding and cutting colors as needed *(see Following A Chart, page 35)*.

Using MC, knit 1{2, 7} rnd(s).

CROWN SHAPING

Work remainder of hat with MC, changing to double pointed needles as needed *(see Double Pointed Needles, page 36)*.

Rnd 1: ★ K8, K2 tog; repeat from ★ to end of rnd: 90{99, 108} sts total.

Rnds 2 and 3: Knit to end of rnd.

Rnd 4: ★ K7, K2 tog; repeat from ★ to end of rnd: 80{88, 96} sts total.

Rnd 5: Knit to end of rnd.

Rnd 6: ★ K6, K2 tog; repeat from ★ to end of rnd: 70{77, 84} sts total.

Rnd 7: Knit to end of rnd.

Rnd 8: ★ K5, K2 tog; repeat from ★ to end of rnd: 60{66, 72} sts total.

Rnd 9: Knit to end of rnd.

Rnd 10: ★ K4, K2 tog; repeat from ★ to end of rnd: 50{55, 60} sts total.

Rnds 11 and 12: Knit to end of rnd.

Rnd 13: ★ K3, K2 tog; repeat from ★ to end of rnd: 40{44, 48} sts total.

Rnd 14: Knit to end of rnd.

Rnd 15: ★ K2, K2 tog; repeat from ★ to end of rnd: 30{33, 36} sts total.

Rnd 16: Knit to end of rnd.

Rnd 17: ★ K1, K2 tog; repeat from ★ to end of rnd: 20{22, 24} sts total.

Rnd 18: Knit to end of rnd.

Rnd 19: ★ K2 tog; repeat from ★ to end of rnd: 10{11, 12} sts total.

Rnd 20: Knit to end of rnd.

FINISHING

Cut yarn leaving an 8" (20.5 cm) end. Thread yarn needle with end and slip remaining sts onto yarn needle and yarn; pull tight to close and secure end.

TIE

With **right** side of one Ear Flap facing, using double pointed needles and MC, pick up 3 sts centered on the cast on edge *(Fig. 11, page 39)*.

Do **not** turn, slide the sts to the opposite end of the needle; ★ K3, do **not** turn, slide the sts to the opposite end of the needle; repeat from ★ until the Tie measures approximately 10" (25.5 cm).

Bind off all sts.

Tie a knot in the end of the cord.

Repeat for second Tie.

Weave in all loose yarn ends.

Block Hat *(see Blocking, page 39)*.

Columbia River Ear Flap Hat

Key

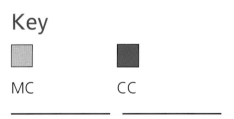

MC   CC

CHART

- 21

- 1

Autumn Beanie

Project: ◧■□□ EASY
Fair Isle pattern: ●●●○ INTERMEDIATE

This is a fitted beanie for those chilly fall days. It has a small Fair Isle pattern with color stripes that blend into one another to help you develop your skill.

Size: Fits head circumference of
19" to 20"{21" to 22"}/
48.5 cm to 51 cm {53.5 cm to 56 cm}

Size Note: Instructions are given for the smallest size with the largest size in braces { }. When only one number is given, it applies to both sizes.

version 2

MATERIALS
Light Weight Yarn
Version 1
[1.75 ounces, 103 yards
(50 grams, 94 meters) per ball]:
  One ball **each** of the following colors:
  MC (Navy), CC1 (Blue), CC2 (Grey),
  CC3 (Burgundy)
Version 2
[1.75 ounces, 164 yards
(50 grams, 150 meters) per hank]:
  One hank **each** of the following colors:
  MC (Brown), CC1 (Ginger), CC2 (Gold),
  CC3 (Burgundy)
16" (40.5 cm) length circular knitting needle,
  size 4 (3.5 mm) **or** size needed for gauge
Set of 4 double pointed knitting needles in
  6" (15 cm) length, size 4 (3.5 mm) **or** size
  needed for gauge
Marker
Tapestry needle

GAUGE: In color pattern,
        28 sts and 32 rnds = 4" (10 cm)

Gauge Swatch:
Cast on 34 sts with MC using a double pointed needle.
Work all right side rows for 32 rows *(see Fair Isle Gauge Swatch, page 35)*.
Bind off all sts.

Techniques used:
• M1 *(Figs. 7a & b, page 38)*
• K2 tog *(Fig. 9, page 38)*

RIBBING

Cast on 120{132} sts with MC using your circular needle.

You will join and begin working in the round. Place a marker before the first stitch to mark the beginning of the round *(see Markers, page 35)*, and make sure that the cast on stitches are not twisted *(see Circular Needles, page 36)*.

Rnds 1-8: ★ P2/MC, K2/CC3; repeat from ★ to end of rnd.

BODY

Rnd 1: Knit with MC to end of rnd.

Rnd 2 (Increase rnd): With MC, ★ K12{16}, M1, K12{17} M1; repeat from ★ to end of rnd: 130{140} sts total.

Rnd 3: Knit with MC to end of rnd.

Rnds 4-38: Knit each rnd following Chart, page 19, from right to left, adding and cutting colors as needed *(see Following A Chart, page 35)*.

CROWN SHAPING

Work remainder of beanie with MC, changing to double pointed needles as needed *(see Double Pointed Needles, page 36)*.

Rnd 1: Using MC, ★ K 11{12}, K2 tog; repeat from ★ to end of rnd: 120{130} sts total.

Rnd 2: Knit to end of rnd.

Rnd 3: ★ K 10{11}, K2 tog; repeat from ★ to end of rnd: 110{120} sts total.

Rnd 4: Knit to end of rnd.

Rnd 5: ★ K9{10}, K2 tog; repeat from ★ to end of rnd: 100{110} sts total.

Rnd 6: Knit to end of rnd.

Rnd 7: ★ K8{9}, K2 tog; repeat from ★ to end of rnd: 90{100} sts total.

Rnd 8: Knit to end of rnd.

Rnd 9: ★ K7{8}, K2 tog; repeat from ★ to end of rnd: 80{90} sts total.

Rnd 10: Knit to end of rnd.

Rnd 11: ★ K6{7}, K2 tog; repeat from ★ to end of rnd: 70{80} sts total.

Rnd 12: ★ K5{6}, K2 tog; repeat from ★ to end of rnd: 60{70} sts total.

Rnd 13: ★ K4{5}, K2 tog; repeat from ★ to end of rnd: 50{60} sts total.

Rnd 14: ★ K3{4}, K2 tog; repeat from ★ to end of rnd: 40{50} sts total.

Rnd 15: ★ K2{3}, K2 tog; repeat from ★ to end of rnd: 30{40} sts total.

Rnd 16: ★ K1{2}, K2 tog; repeat from ★ to end of rnd: 20{30} sts total.

LARGEST SIZE ONLY - Rnd 17: ★ K1, K2 tog; repeat from ★ to end of rnd: 20 sts total.

BOTH SIZES - Last Rnd: ★ K2 tog; repeat from ★ to end of rnd: 10 sts total.

Cut yarn leaving an 8" (20.5 cm) end. Thread tapestry needle with end and slip remaining sts onto tapestry needle and yarn; pull tight to close and secure end.

Weave in all loose yarn ends.

Block Beanie *(see Blocking, page 39)*.

Autumn Beanie

Key

⬛	🟫	🟨	🟧
MC	CC1	CC2	CC3

CHART

- 38

- 4

isure Arts grants you permission to make a color copy of this page. Write the color yarns you're using under the key. Cut sample of yarn and tape it under the color.

t the page on a chart holder and lay a magnet on it to keep your place. The chart holder can be inserted in a page otector with the magnet on the outside, if desired.

Little Sophia's Hat

Project: ◖◼◻◻ **EASY**
Fair Isle pattern: ●●●○ **INTERMEDIATE +**

This is a stylish hat for a little one. It contains a colorful Fair Isle pattern just for fun. Eyelets are made at the top of the hat. One forms a picot edge, and the other provides a place to weave a colorful, twisted cord through to gather and shape the hat.

Child Size: Fits 12-18 months {18-24 months, 2-3 years}

Size Note: Instructions are given for size 12-18 months with sizes 18-24 months and 2-3 years in braces { }. When only one number is given, it applies to all sizes.

version 1

MATERIALS

Light Weight Yarn

Version 1
[1.75 ounces, 164 yards (50 grams, 150 meters) per hank]:
   One hank **each** of the following colors:
   MC (Blue), CC1 (Lt Blue), CC2 (Orange), CC3 (Gold), CC4 (Magenta)

Version 2
[1.75 ounces, 137 yards (50 grams, 125 meters) per ball]:
   One ball **each** of the following colors:
   MC (Green), CC1 (Lt Green), CC2 (Yellow), CC3 (Blue), CC4 (Rose)

16" (40.5 cm) length circular knitting needle, size 4 (3.5 mm) **or** size needed for gauge

Set of 4 double pointed knitting needles in 6" (15 cm) length, size 4 (3.5 mm) **or** size needed for gauge

Marker

Yarn and tapestry needles

GAUGE: In color pattern,
   28 sts and 32 rnds = 4" (10 cm)

Gauge Swatch:
Cast on 36 sts with CC1 using a double pointed needle.
Work all right side rows for 32 rows *(see Fair Isle Gauge Swatch, page 35).*
Bind off all sts.

Techniques used:
• YO *(Fig. 6, page 38)*
• K2 tog *(Fig. 9, page 38)*

RIBBING

Cast on 96{112, 128} sts with MC using your circular needle.

You will join and begin working in the round. Place a marker before the first stitch to mark the beginning of the round *(see Markers, page 35)*, and make sure that the cast on stitches are not twisted *(see Circular Needles, page 36)*.

Rnd 1: ★ P2/MC, K2/CC4; repeat from ★ to end of rnd.

Repeat Rnd 1 for a total of 5{7, 7} rnds.

BODY

Rnds 1-41: Knit each rnd following Chart, page 23, from right to left, adding and cutting colors as needed *(see Following A Chart, page 35)*.

CROWN SHAPING

Work remainder of hat with MC, changing to double pointed needles as needed *(see Double Pointed Needles, page 36)*.

SIZE 12-18 MONTHS ONLY
Rnd 1: Knit to end of rnd.

Rnd 2: ★ K2, K2 tog; repeat from ★ to end of rnd: 72 sts total.

Rnd 3: Knit to end of rnd.

Rnd 4: ★ K1, K2 tog; repeat from ★ to end of rnd: 48 sts total.

Rnd 5: Knit to end of rnd.

Rnd 6: ★ K2 tog; repeat from ★ to end of rnd: 24 sts total.

Eyelet Rnd: ★ YO, K2 tog; repeat from ★ to end of rnd.

SIZES 18-24 MONTHS & 2-3 YEARS ONLY
Rnds 1 and 2: Knit to end of rnd.

Rnd 3: ★ K2, K2 tog; repeat from ★ to end of rnd: {84, 96} sts total.

Rnds 4-6: Knit to end of rnd.

Rnd 7: ★ K1, K2 tog; repeat from ★ to end of rnd: {56, 64} sts total.

Rnd 8: Knit to end of rnd.

Rnd 9: ★ K2 tog; repeat from ★ to end of rnd: {28, 32} sts total.

Eyelet Rnd: ★ YO, K2 tog; repeat from ★ to end of rnd.

ALL SIZES
Knit 6{6, 7} rnds.

Eyelet Rnd: ★ YO, K2 tog; repeat from ★ to end of rnd.

Knit 5{4, 6} rnds.

Bind off remaining sts loosely.

FINISHING
Fold top edge at last Eyelet Rnd made, forming picot edge, and sew bound off sts in place above first Eyelet Rnd.

Weave in all loose yarn ends.

Block Hat *(see Blocking, page 39)*.

TWISTED CORD
Cut a 40" (101.5 cm) length from each of the 4 contrasting colors.

Holding all 4 strands together, fold the four strands in half. Tie a loose knot at each end. Fasten one end to a stationary object or have another person hold it; insert a knitting needle at the opposite end, making sure that there are 4 strands of yarn on either side of needle. Turn the knitting needle end so that you're twisting the yarn together. Continue to turn until the yarn is tightly twisted.

Leaving the knitting needle in the end, remove the other end from the chair, holding both ends so that the cord doesn't unwind. Thread yarn needle with the strands above the knot and carefully thread this cord through the Eyelets on the top of the hat. Once you reach the last hole, draw up the hat and even up the ends until they match.

Holding both ends together, remove the knitting needle and release the hat, allowing the yarn to twist back on itself. Keeping the cords twisted, knot the ends together. Remove the previous knots you made, and clip the looped ends. You now have a tassel.

To close the opening at the top of the hat, you will use a weaving technique, working in the stitches just above the bound off edge, as follows:

Thread tapestry needle with MC. Fold the hat in half along the top edge. Insert the needle from right to left under the legs of the stitch on the top edge *(Fig. 2a)*, then under the inverted V of the next stitch on the bottom edge *(Fig. 2b)*. Continue across, pulling the yarn gently every 2 or 3 stitches and being careful to maintain even tension. Weave in yarn ends.

Fig. 2a

Fig. 2b

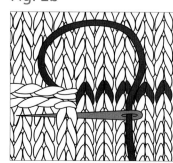

Little Sophia's Hat

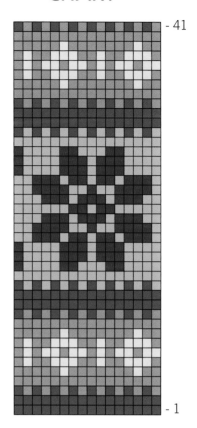

- 41

- 1

Key

MC   CC1   CC2   CC3   CC4

_____   _____   _____   _____   _____

Leisure Arts grants you permission to make a color copy of this page. Write the color yarns you're using under the key. Cut a sample of yarn and tape it under the color.

Put the page on a chart holder and lay a magnet on it to keep your place. The chart holder can be inserted in a page protector with the magnet on the outside, if desired.

Ginger's Slouch Hat

Project: ■■□□ EASY +

Fair Isle pattern: ●●●● EXPERIENCED

This stylish hat is made with a super fine weight yarn that allows the knit fabric to drape well. It has many color changes for practicing your technique and to add more interest from top to bottom. It begins with lots of color in the ribbing and ends with a small Fair Isle pattern in the crown shaping.

Size: Fits head circumference of 20" to 23" (51 cm to 58.5 cm)

version 2

MATERIALS

Super Fine Weight Yarn

Version 1

[1.75 ounces, 231 yards (50 grams, 211 meters) per ball]:
  One ball **each** of the following colors:
  MC (Red), CC1 (Gold), CC2 (Lt Gold), CC3 (Dk Blue), CC4 (Blue), CC5 (Lt Blue)

Version 2

[.88 ounces, 115 yards (25 grams, 105 meters) per skein]:
  One skein **each** of the following colors:
  MC (Maroon), CC1 (Rose), CC2 (Lt Rose), CC3 (Dk Green), CC4 (Green), CC5 (Lt Green)

16" (40.5 cm) length circular knitting needle, size 3 (3.25 mm) **or** size needed for gauge

Set of 4 double pointed knitting needles in 6" (15 cm) length, size 3 (3.25 mm) **or** size needed for gauge

Markers - 9

Tapestry needle

GAUGE: In color pattern, 32 sts and 40 rnds = 4" (10 cm)

Gauge Swatch:
Cast on 44 sts with MC using a double pointed needle.
Work all right side rows for 40 rows *(see Fair Isle Gauge Swatch, page 35)*.
Bind off all sts.

Techniques used:
- M1 *(Figs. 7a & b, page 38)*
- K2 tog *(Fig. 9, page 38)*
- SSK *(Figs. 10a-c, page 39)*

RIBBING

Cast on 140 sts with MC using your circular needle.

You will join and begin working in the round. Place a marker before the first stitch to mark the beginning of the round *(see Markers, page 35)*, and make sure that the cast on stitches are not twisted *(see Circular Needles, page 36)*.

The Ribbing can be made following the written instructions or by following the Ribbing Chart on page 29 *(see Following A Chart, page 35)*. Choose whichever is easiest for you.

Rnds 1 and 2: ★ P2/MC, K2/CC5; repeat from ★ to end of rnd.

Rnd 3: Cut MC, join CC1, ★ P2/CC1, K2/CC5; repeat from ★ to end of rnd.

Rnd 4: ★ P2/CC1, K2/CC5; repeat from ★ to end of rnd.

Rnd 5: Cut CC5, join CC4, ★ P2/CC1, K2/CC4; repeat from ★ to end of rnd.

Rnd 6: ★ P2/CC1, K2/CC4; repeat from ★ to end of rnd.

Rnd 7: Cut CC1, join CC2, ★ P2/CC2, K2/CC4; repeat from ★ to end of rnd.

Rnd 8: ★ P2/CC2, K2/CC4; repeat from ★ to end of rnd.

Rnd 9: Cut CC4, join CC3, ★ P2/CC2, K2/CC3; repeat from ★ to end of rnd.

Rnd 10: ★ P2/CC2, K2/CC3; repeat from ★ to end of rnd.

Rnd 11: Cut CC2, join MC, ★ P2/MC, K2/CC3; repeat from ★ to end of rnd.

Rnd 12: ★ P2/MC, K2/CC3; repeat from ★ to end of rnd.

Cut CC3.

BODY

Rnd 1: Knit with MC to end of rnd.

Rnd 2 (Increase rnd): ★ K3, M1, K4, M1; repeat from ★ to end of rnd placing a marker after every 20 sts to indicate pattern repeat (use a different colored marker than for the beginning of the round): 180 sts total and 9 pattern repeats.

Rnds 3-56: Knit each rnd following Main Pattern Chart, page 29, from right to left, cutting and joining colors as needed *(see Floats, page 36)*.

Cut CC5.

CROWN SHAPING

Change to double pointed needles as needed *(see Double Pointed Needles, page 36)*.

Rnd 1: Knit with CC3 to end of rnd.

Rnd 2: ★ K1, K2 tog, K 15, SSK; repeat from ★ to end of rnd: 162 sts total.

Rnd 3: Knit to end of rnd.

Rnd 4: ★ K1, K2 tog, K 13, SSK; repeat from ★ to end of rnd: 144 sts total.

Rnd 5: Knit to end of rnd.

Rnd 6: Join CC4, ★ K1/CC4, K1/CC3; repeat from ★ to end of rnd; cut CC3.

Rnd 7: Using CC4, ★ K1, K2 tog, K 11, SSK; repeat from ★ to end of rnd: 126 sts total.

Rnd 8: Knit to end of rnd.

Rnd 9: ★ K1, K2 tog, K9, SSK; repeat from ★ to end of rnd: 108 sts total.

Rnd 10: Knit to end of rnd.

Rnd 11: ★ K1, K2 tog, K7, SSK; repeat from ★ to end of rnd: 90 sts total.

Rnd 12: Join CC1, K1/CC1, K3/CC4, ★ K2/CC1, K3/CC4; repeat from ★ to last st, K1/CC1.

Rnd 13: K2/CC1, K1/CC4, ★ K4/CC1, K1/CC4; repeat from ★ to last 2 sts, K2/CC1.

Rnd 14: K1/CC1, K3/CC4, ★ K2/CC1, K3/CC4; repeat from ★ to last st, K1/CC1; cut CC1.

Rnd 15: Using CC4, ★ K1, K2 tog, K5, SSK; repeat from ★ to end of rnd: 72 sts total.

Rnd 16: Join CC3, ★ K1/CC4, K1/CC3; repeat from ★ to end of rnd; cut CC4.

Rnd 17: Using CC3, ★ K1, K2 tog, K3, SSK; repeat from ★ to end of rnd: 54 sts total.

Rnd 18: Knit to end of rnd.

Rnd 19: ★ K1, K2 tog, K1, SSK; repeat from ★ to end of rnd: 36 sts total.

Rnd 20: Knit to end of rnd.

Close top of hat with three needle bind off as follows:

Divide sts, placing 18 sts on each of 2 double pointed needles. Holding piece with **right** side together and needles parallel to each other, insert a third needle as if to **knit** into the first stitch on the front needle **and** into the first stitch on the back needle *(Fig. 3)*. Knit these two stitches together and slip them off the needle.
★ Knit the next stitch on each needle together and slip them off the needle. To bind off, insert one of the left needles into the first stitch on the right needle and pull the first stitch over the second stitch and off the right needle; repeat from ★ across until all of the stitches have been bound off. Cut yarn and pull through remaining loop.

Fig. 3

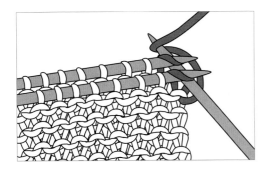

Weave in all loose yarn ends.

Block Hat *(see Blocking, page 39)*.

Ginger's Slouch Hat

MAIN PATTERN CHART

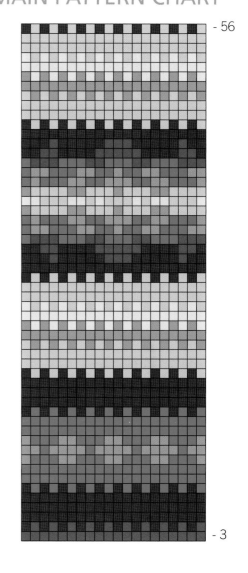

- 56

- 3

RIBBING CHART

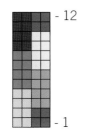

- 12

- 1

Note: Work in 2x2 (P2, K2) ribbing.

Key

 MC

 CC1

 CC2

 CC3

 CC4

CC5

Cranberry Rose Hat

Project: ◖■□□ **EASY**

Fair Isle pattern: ●●●● **EXPERIENCED**

This classy hat uses six colors to "paint" the ribbing and includes small and large shaded designs.

Size: Fits head circumference of 20" to 22" (51 cm to 56 cm)

MATERIALS

Light Weight Yarn 🧶 **LIGHT 3**
[1.75 ounces, 164 yards
(50 grams, 150 meters) per hank]:
   One hank **each** of the following colors:
   MC (Dk Plum), CC1 (Magenta), CC2 (Rose),
   CC3 (Green), CC4 (Lt Green), CC5 (Pink)
16" (40.5 cm) length circular knitting needle,
   size 4 (3.5 mm) **or** size needed for gauge
Set of 4 double pointed knitting needles in
   6" (15 cm) length, size 4 (3.5 mm) **or** size
   needed for gauge
Markers - 7
Tapestry needle

GAUGE: In color pattern,
           28 sts and 32 rnds = 4" (10 cm)

Gauge Swatch:
Cast on 48 sts with CC3 using a double pointed needle.
Work all right side rows for 32 rows *(see Fair Isle Gauge Swatch, page 35)*.
Bind off all sts.

Techniques used:
• M1 *(Figs. 7a & b, page 38)*
• K2 tog *(Fig. 9, page 38)*

RIBBING
Cast on 140 sts with MC using your circular needle.

You will join and begin working in the round. Place a marker before the first stitch to mark the beginning of the round *(see Markers, page 35)*, and make sure that the cast on stitches are not twisted *(see Circular Needles, page 36)*.

The Ribbing can be made following the written instructions on page 31 or by following the Ribbing Chart on page 33 *(see Following A Chart, page 35)*. Choose whichever is easiest for you.

Rnds 1 and 2: ★ P2/MC, K2/CC4; repeat from ★ to end of rnd.

Rnd 3: Cut MC, join CC1, ★ P2/CC1, K2/CC4; repeat from ★ to end of rnd.

Rnd 4: ★ P2/CC1, K2/CC4; repeat from ★ to end of rnd.

Rnd 5: Cut CC4, join CC3, ★ P2/CC1, K2/CC3; repeat from ★ to end of rnd.

Rnd 6: ★ P2/CC1, K2/CC3; repeat from ★ to end of rnd.

Rnd 7: Cut CC1, join CC2, ★ P2/CC2, K2/CC3; repeat from ★ to end of rnd.

Rnd 8: ★ P2/CC2, K2/CC3; repeat from ★ to end of rnd.

Rnd 9: Cut CC3, join CC5, ★ P2/CC2, K2/CC5; repeat from ★ to end of rnd.

Rnd 10: ★ P2/CC2, K2/CC5; repeat from ★ to end of rnd.

Rnd 11: Cut CC2, join MC, ★ P2/MC, K2/CC5; repeat from ★ to end of rnd.

Rnd 12: ★ P2/MC, K2/CC5; repeat from ★ to end of rnd.

Cut CC5.

BODY

Rnd 1: Knit with MC to end of rnd.

Rnd 2 (Increase rnd): ★ K 10, M1; repeat from ★ to end of rnd placing a marker after every 22 sts to indicate pattern repeat (use a different colored marker than for the beginning of the round): 154 sts total and 7 pattern repeats.

Rnds 3-50: Knit each rnd following Main Pattern Chart, page 35, from right to left, cutting and joining colors as needed *(see Floats, page 36)*.

CROWN SHAPING

Work remainder of hat with MC, changing to double pointed needles as needed *(see Double Pointed Needles, page 36)*.

Rnd 1: ★ K5, K2 tog; repeat from ★ to end of rnd: 132 sts total.

Rnd 2: Knit to end of rnd.

Rnd 3: ★ K 10, K2 tog; repeat from ★ to end of rnd: 121 sts total.

Rnd 4: Knit to end of rnd.

Rnd 5: ★ K9, K2 tog; repeat from ★ to end of rnd: 110 sts total.

Rnd 6: Knit to end of rnd.

Rnd 7: ★ K8, K2 tog; repeat from ★ to end of rnd: 99 sts total.

Rnd 8: Knit to end of rnd.

Rnd 9: ★ K7, K2 tog; repeat from ★ to end of rnd: 88 sts total.

Rnd 10: ★ K6, K2 tog; repeat from ★ to end of rnd: 77 sts total.

Rnd 11: ★ K5, K2 tog; repeat from ★ to end of rnd: 66 sts total.

Rnd 12: ★ K4, K2 tog; repeat from ★ to end of rnd: 55 sts total.

Rnd 13: ★ K3, K2 tog; repeat from ★ to end of rnd: 44 sts total.

Rnd 14: ★ K2, K2 tog; repeat from ★ to end of rnd: 33 sts total.

Rnd 15: ★ K1, K2 tog; repeat from ★ to end of rnd: 22 sts total.

Rnd: 16: ★ K2 tog; repeat from ★ to end of rnd: 11 sts total.

Cut yarn leaving an 8" (20.5 cm) end. Thread tapestry needle with end and slip remaining sts onto tapestry needle and yarn; pull up tight to close and secure end.

Weave in all loose yarn ends.

Block Hat *(see Blocking, page 39)*.

Cranberry Rose Hat

MAIN PATTERN CHART

- 50

- 3

RIBBING CHART

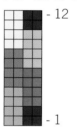

- 12

- 1

Note: Work in 2x2 (P2, K2) ribbing.

Key

MC

CC1

CC2

CC3

CC4

CC5

ABBREVIATIONS

CC	Contrasting Color
cm	centimeters
K	knit
M1	make one
M1P	make one purl
MC	Main Color
mm	millimeters
P	purl
Rnd(s)	Round(s)
SSK	slip, slip, knit
st(s)	stitch(es)
tog	together
YO	yarn over

★ — work instructions following ★ as many **more** times as indicated in addition to the first time.

( ) or [ ] — contains explanatory remarks.

colon (:) — the number(s) given after a colon at the end of a row or round denote(s) the number of stitches you should have on that row or round.

KNIT TERMINOLOGY	
UNITED STATES	**INTERNATIONAL**
gauge =	tension
bind off =	cast off
yarn over (YO) =	yarn forward (yfwd) **or** yarn around needle (yrn)

◼◻◻◻ BEGINNER	Projects for first-time knitters using basic knit and purl stitches. Minimal shaping.
◼◼◻◻ EASY	Projects using basic stitches, repetitive stitch patterns, simple color changes, and simple shaping and finishing.
◼◼◼◻ INTERMEDIATE	Projects with a variety of stitches, such as basic cables and lace, simple intarsia, double-pointed needles and knitting in the round needle techniques, mid-level shaping and finishing.
◼◼◼◼ EXPERIENCED	Projects using advanced techniques and stitches, such as short rows, fair isle, more intricate intarsia, cables, lace patterns, and numerous color changes.

Yarn Weight Symbol & Names	LACE 0	SUPER FINE 1	FINE 2	LIGHT 3	MEDIUM 4	BULKY 5	SUPER BULKY 6
Type of Yarns in Category	Fingering, size 10 crochet thread	Sock, Fingering, Baby	Sport, Baby	DK, Light Worsted	Worsted, Afghan, Aran	Chunky, Craft, Rug	Bulky, Roving
Knit Gauge Range* in Stockinette St to 4" (10 cm)	33-40** sts	27-32 sts	23-26 sts	21-24 sts	16-20 sts	12-15 sts	6-11 sts
Advised Needle Size Range	000-1	1 to 3	3 to 5	5 to 7	7 to 9	9 to 11	11 and larger

*GUIDELINES ONLY: The chart above reflects the most commonly used gauges and needle sizes for specific yarn categories.

** Lace weight yarns are usually knitted on larger needles to create lacy openwork patterns. Accordingly, a gauge range is difficult to determine. Always follow the gauge stated in your pattern.

KNITTING NEEDLES

UNITED STATES	ENGLISH U.K.	METRIC (mm)
0	13	2
1	12	2.25
2	11	2.75
3	10	3.25
4	9	3.5
5	8	3.75
6	7	4
7	6	4.5
8	5	5
9	4	5.5
10	3	6
10½	2	6.5
11	1	8
13	00	9
15	000	10
17	---	12.75

GAUGE

Exact gauge is essential for proper fit. Before beginning your project, make a sample swatch in the yarn and needle specified in the individual instructions *(see Fair Isle Gauge Swatch, below)*. After completing the swatch, measure it, counting your stitches and rows carefully. If your swatch is larger or smaller than specified, make another, changing needle size to get the correct gauge. **Keep trying until you find the size needles that will give you the specified gauge.**

FAIR ISLE GAUGE SWATCH

Exact gauge is essential when making a garment that needs to fit properly, such as a hat. It is important to make a gauge swatch in the color pattern following the chart. Since the projects are worked in the round with the right side facing, you will need to make a flat swatch with all right side rows.

Using double pointed needles, cast on the number of stitches indicated for the Gauge Swatch in the individual project.

Row 1 (Right side): Knit across.

Begin following the main color pattern chart starting with the first row that uses two colors.

Row 2 (Right side): Do **not** turn, slide the sts to the opposite end of the needle, bring the working yarn loosely across the wrong side; K1 holding both colors together, K1 using background color, knit across following chart to the last 2 sts, K1 using background color, K1 holding both colors together.

Follow the chart for the number of rows specified in the gauge swatch, always working with the **right** side facing and working the edge stitches with both colors on every 2-color row.

Bind off.

After completing the swatch, measure the number of stitches specified for the gauge. If it measures larger or smaller than specified, make another swatch, changing the needle size to get the correct gauge. **Keep trying until you find the size needles that will give you the specified gauge.**

FOLLOWING A CHART

Projects for Fair Isle knitting are usually made by following a chart for the main color pattern. The written instructions are given for all of the ribbings. A chart is also given for Ginger's Slouch Hat, page 29, and Cranberry Rose Hat, page 33, since the ribbings have many color changes. When following a chart for the ribbing, the purl stitches are not indicated on the chart since the chart is for color purposes only.

The chart shows each stitch as a square, indicating what color each stitch should be. Visualize the chart as your fabric, beginning at the bottom edge. More than one pattern repeat may be given on the main color pattern chart so you can easily see the pattern. Since you are knitting in the round, **always follow the chart from right to left.**

Place your magnet right **above** the row you are knitting because you will want to see the round you have just completed. This will ensure you are working the correct color.

MARKERS

As a convenience to you, we have used markers to help distinguish the beginning of a round and to indicate the pattern repeats. Place markers as instructed. You may use purchased markers or tie a length of contrasting color yarn around the needle. When you reach a marker on each round, slip it from the left needle to the right needle; remove it when no longer needed.

CIRCULAR NEEDLES

When you knit a tube, as for a cowl or a hat, you are going to work around on the outside of the circle with the right side of the knitting facing you. Using a circular needle, cast on all stitches as instructed. Untwist and straighten the stitches on the needle to be sure that the cast on ridge lays on the inside of the needle and never rolls around the needle.

Hold the needle so that the ball of yarn is attached to the stitch closest to the right hand point. Place a marker on the right hand point to mark the beginning of the round.

To begin working in the round, work the stitches on the left hand point *(Fig. 4)*.

Continue working each round as instructed without turning the work; but for the first three rounds or so, check to be sure that the cast on edge has not twisted around the needle. If it has, it is impossible to untwist it. The only way to fix this is to rip it out and return to the cast on row.

Fig. 4

DOUBLE POINTED NEEDLES

When working too few stitches to use a circular needle, double pointed needles are required. Divide the stitches into thirds and slip one-third of the stitches onto each of 3 double pointed needles, forming a triangle. With the fourth needle, knit across the stitches on the first needle *(Fig. 5)*. You will now have an empty needle with which to knit the stitches from the next needle. Work the first stitch of each needle firmly to prevent gaps.

Fig. 5

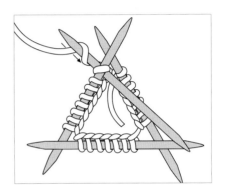

FLOATS

When working a large section of color, the **floats** *(the yarn carried across the back)* become too long to easily keep tension. The yarn can be caught at its midpoint with the yarn in use. Catch the yarn float every three or four stitches. A rule of thumb is never to carry the yarn more than one inch *(Photo 10)*. Also, never catch the float on the first or last stitch of a color change.

Photo 10

When knitting 3 or more consecutive background stitches with the right hand yarn, insert the right hand needle into the next stitch and bring the left yarn (dominant) forward over the right hand needle tip (clockwise) *(Photo 11)*. Bring the right yarn (background) from under and then over the tip of the right needle (counterclockwise) *(Photo 12)*, then move the left yarn off the needle and complete the stitch. The left yarn is now on top of the right yarn and will be anchored when you knit the next stitch. Be careful not to tighten the tension and also make sure the carried yarn doesn't show on the right side.

When knitting 3 or more consecutive dominant stitches with the left hand yarn, insert the right hand needle into the next stitch, bring the right yarn (background) forward from under and then over the right hand needle tip (counterclockwise) *(Photo 13)*. Bring the left yarn (dominant) forward from under and then over the right hand needle tip (counterclockwise) *(Photo 14)*, then move the right yarn off the needle and complete the stitch.

Photo 11

Photo 12

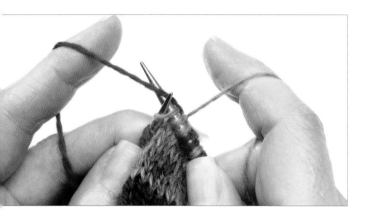

Photo 13

Photo 14

YARN OVER (abbreviated YO)

Bring the yarn forward **between** the needles, then back **over** the top of the right hand needle, so that it is now in position to knit the next stitch **(Fig. 6)**.

Fig. 6

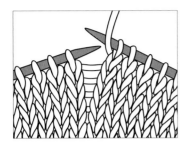

MAKE ONE (abbreviated M1)

Insert the left needle under the horizontal strand between the stitches from the **front (Fig. 7a)**. Then **knit** into the **back** of the strand **(Fig. 7b)**.

Fig. 7a   Fig. 7b

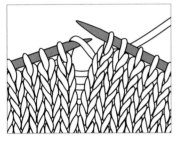   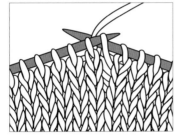

MAKE ONE PURL (abbreviated M1P)

Insert the left needle under the horizontal strand between the stitches from the **back (Fig. 8a)**. Then **purl** into the **front** of the strand **(Fig. 8b)**.

Fig. 8a   Fig. 8b

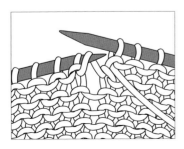   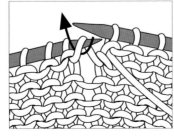

KNIT 2 TOGETHER (abbreviated K2 tog)

Insert the right needle into the **front** of the first two stitches on the left needle as if to **knit (Fig. 9)**, then **knit** them together as if they were one stitch.

Fig. 9

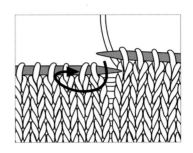

SLIP, SLIP, KNIT (abbreviated SSK)

Separately slip two stitches as if to **knit (Fig. 10a)**. Insert the left needle into the **front** of both slipped stitches **(Fig. 10b)**, then **knit** them together as if they were one stitch **(Fig. 10c)**.

Fig. 10a   Fig. 10b

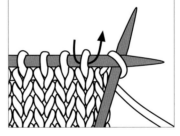   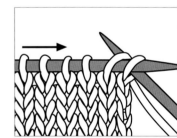

Fig. 10c

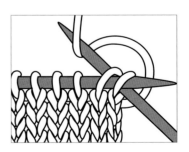

PICKING UP STITCHES

When instructed to pick up stitches, insert the needle from the **front** to the **back** under two strands at the edge of the worked piece *(Fig. 11)*. Put the yarn around the needle as if to **knit**, then bring the needle with the yarn back through the stitch to the right side, resulting in a stitch on the needle.

Repeat this along the edge, picking up the required number of stitches.

Fig. 11

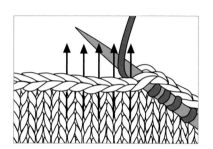

BLOCKING

Check the yarn label for any special instructions about blocking. Place your project on a clean terry towel over a flat surface and shape it to size. A cloth can be placed inside the cowl or hat to prevent creases at the sides. Place a damp cloth on top and hold a handheld steamer or steam iron just above the item and steam it thoroughly. Never let the weight of the iron touch the item because it will flatten the stitches. Allow the item to dry flat, away from heat or sunlight.

We have made every effort to ensure that these instructions are accurate and complete. We cannot, however, be responsible for human error, typographical mistakes, or variations in individual work.

PRODUCTION TEAM:
Writer/Technical Editor - Cathy Hardy
Editorial Writer - Susan McManus Johnson
Graphic Artists - Katherine Laughlin and Becca Snider
Photo Stylists - Angela Alexander and Sondra Daniel
Photographers - Jason Masters and Ken West

YARN INFORMATION

The cowl and hats in this leaflet were made using a variety of yarns and weights. Any brand of the specific weight of yarn may be used. It is best to refer to the yardage/meters when determining how many skeins, balls, or hanks to purchase. Remember, to arrive at the finished size, it is the GAUGE/TENSION that is important, not the brand of yarn.

For your convenience, listed below are the specific yarns used to create our photography models.

GARDEN COWL
Version #1
Knit Picks® Wool of the Andes Worsted
MC - #24077 Dove Heather
CC1 - #25075 Rouge
CC2 - #23439 Grass
CC3 - #24275 Fairy Tale

Version #2
Patons® Classic Wool
MC - #00208 Burgundy
CC1 - #00210 Petal Pink
CC2 - #77208 Jade Heather
CC3 - #00218 Peacock

COLUMBIA RIVER EAR FLAP HAT
Version #1
Patons® Classic Wool
MC - #00224 Grey Mix
CC - #77132 Royal Blue

Version #2
Lion Brand® Lion® Wool
MC - #123 Sage
CC - #140 Rose

AUTUMN BEANIE
Version #1
Knit Picks Telemark
MC - #25041 Navy
CC1 - #23927 Alpine Frost
CC2 - #25039 Dove Heather
CC3 - #24025 Garnet Heather

Version #2
Cascade Yarns 220 Sport
MC - #9408 Cordovan
CC1 - #2414 Ginger
CC2 - #7827 Goldenrod
CC3 - #2401 Burgundy

LITTLE SOPHIA'S HAT
Version #1
Cascade Yarns 220 Sport
MC - #8891 Cyan Blue
CC1 - #8906 Blue Topaz
CC2 - #7824 Burnt Orange
CC3 - #7827 Goldenrod
CC4 - #7803 Magenta

Version #2
Universal Yarn® Debbie Macomber Blossom Street™ Collection, Rosebud
MC - #507 Clover
CC1 - #508 Tendril
CC2 - #509 Honeysuckle
CC3 - #506 Bachelor Button
CC4 - #501 Bleeding Heart

GINGER'S SLOUCH HAT
Version #1
Knit Picks® Palette
MC - #24553 Serrano
CC1 - #24251 Turmeric
CC2 - #24250 Semolina
CC3 - #24581 Jay
CC4 - #24582 Celestial
CC5 - #24578 Bluebell

Version #2
Jamieson's Shetland Spindrift
MC - #595 Maroon
CC1 - #570 Sorbet
CC2 - #550 Rose
CC3 - #805 Spruce
CC4 - #772 Verdigris
CC5 - #274 Green Mist

CRANBERRY ROSE HAT
Cascade Yarns 220 Sport
MC - #8885 Dark Plum
CC1 - #7803 Magenta
CC2 - #7802 Cerise
CC3 - #2452 Turtle
CC4 - #8914 Granny Smith
CC5 - #9477 Tutu